Work Perks

A Gratitude Journal For Helping Professionals

Terricka Hardy, LCSW, ACSW, BCD

Work Perks

A Gratitude Journal For Helping Professionals

Why Work Perks?

"Perk" is defined by the Oxford Dictionaries as "money, goods, or other benefits to which one is entitled as an employee or as a shareholder of a company."

Most of the time when we think about work perks, we often think about the money and/or goods that it yields; basically, the tangible. I am in no way saying that those things do not matter. What I am conveying is that often times we place more power in the money and goods (the tangible) while completely forgetting the "OTHER BENEFITS" (the intangible) as a result of the powerful work that you do.

Whether you absolutely love your job, hate it, or have feelings betwixt the two I believe the work that you do have perks that go unnoticed. The truth is that the current position that you are in is helping to shape you into the person you are becoming. It's easy to complain about the challenging work that you do on a daily basis, but if you want to move past the complaining stage...THIS JOURNAL IS FOR YOU. I have had the privilege of presenting to many professionals across the nation. As a mental health professional with years of experience, I know that the work in helping and serving others can be challenging and just plain ole hard. Nevertheless, it has shaped and molded me into the person I am today.

Learning to find the perks in my work has changed my professional perspective and yielded better outcomes professionally and personally. As a result, it has made me a better wife, mom, daughter, sister, friend, and professional.

The goal of this journal is simple. It is my hope that this journal helps you to establish a practice of gratitude, self-reflection, and alleviate the risk of burnout. Through the lenses of gratitude and self-reflection, I am going to teach you what I have taught myself over the years, how to view the challenges you face in your work as actual perks.

The Art of Journaling

Why exactly is journaling important? Simply put, journaling gives you the opportunity to write your way to more positive, healthier thoughts and behaviors. Journaling requires self-reflection. It compels the writer to discover thoughts that often go unnoticed. But journaling doesn't just stop there. It can also transform your thoughts. When you transform the way you think, you can transform your actions.

Gratitude

Why gratitude? The true practice of gratitude is one of the most cost effective, evidenced based strategies that will help to improve your quality of life. The great news is that you can learn it.

Gratitude is more than just writing down three things you are grateful for. This journal goes deeper. It will require you to actually pay attention to YOU. It will require you to be reflective and more self-aware. Most importantly it will challenge you to be skilled at identifying the good things that sometimes come by way of challenges.

What is gratitude? Gratitude is expressing appreciation for what you currently have. Did you know that practicing gratitude has the power to actually change your brain? It's true. According to researcher, Shawn Anchor, the author of The Happiness Advantage, practicing gratitude for at least 21 days has the power to increase your level of optimism for up to 6 months. Simply put, 21 days of practicing gratitude could add six months of positive change to your life. Here's the breakdown, there's approximately 30 to 31 days in each month, with the exception of February. 30 (days) x 6 (months) = approximately 180 days. Based on this research, if you invest 21 days of practicing gratitude, it could yield 180 days of optimism. Sounds like a good deal huh... if you could invest $21 and get a $180 return that would be a no brainer, right?! I'd like for you to think of this journal as an investment tool that could yield an even greater return.

More Perks

Embracing a lifestyle of gratitude has many more perks. Gratitude has been known to increase willpower, help to keep one calm, increase your morale at work, and lower stress. Although it has been known to build morale at work and lower stress levels, many rarely express gratitude at work. If we are aware of the benefits of gratitude then why is it that individuals find it difficult to express gratitude while at work? Just hearing the words "thank you" or feeling appreciated at work has been said to boost happiness, reduce stress, and improve satisfaction. It is often believed that showing gratitude at work can make others think that you are "brown nosing" or "kissing up" to your boss. While others think that showing gratitude may be seen as a weakness, some may view it as an opportunity to give you more work attempting to take advantage of you.

Instead of thinking about the negative things, I challenge you to think about the perks of practicing gratitude could yield to you, personally and professionally.

Burnout

The World Health Organization (WHO) recognizes burnout as a medical diagnosis. WHO defines burnout as an employment related syndrome and has included it in the International Classification of Diseases Handbook (ICD). The ICD handbook is used by medical professionals and health insurers for diagnostic purposes. What does this have to do with this journal and you? A LOT! As a professional that has been researching burnout, I've had the privilege of presenting workshops to professionals nationally on burnout and self-care. In my opinion, I don't think burnout awareness is talked about enough. The fact that WHO has included burnout in the ICD Handbook means that the world is beginning to recognize the dangers of burnout. However, one needs to note that according to WHO, burnout has been recategorized as a problem pertaining to employment and/or unemployment. In the updated ICD 11, burnout will be considered an employment related issue that results in chronic workplace stress.

The signs of burnout can be associated with feelings of exhaustion, energy depletion, feeling distance from one's work, negative thoughts/ feelings towards work, and a decrease in professional performance and/or efficacy.

But there is hope. This journal is here to be a resource for you. Whether, you feel as if you are burned out, could possibly be becoming burned out, or attempting to prevent burnout this journal is for you. I know first hand how overwhelming work and life can be. I, too, have experienced symptoms of burnout. I know exactly how it feels to have a love/ hate relationship with your work. I know how it feels to help a client and/or colleague achieve the greatest breakthrough of their lives all while feeling stuck personally and professionally. Burnout, compassion fatigue, and just overall stress is REAL. If you've ever felt that way you don't have to stay there. That is not your end. This journal can help you navigate through it.

Self–Reflection

You will find many self- reflection writing opportunities in this journal. I strategically infused this journal with self- reflection because we don't do it enough. Self- reflection has been shown to be a contributing trait in building resilience. I view self-reflection as giving one the opportunity, time, and space to simply think. Let's face it, life is busy these days. Many of you reading this are wives/ husbands, mothers/ fathers, sisters/ brothers, friends to many, and professionals. You wear MANY hats. Being able to self-reflect about experiences has benefits and is a great form of self-care. And trust me, self-care is needed with the many hats that you wear. With all of the responsibilities you have it's easy to feel stuck and overwhelmed. Self-reflection gives you the opportunity to learn from your experiences and to allow what you learned to inform your future in a positive way. Self- reflection involves thinking and questioning yourself about experiences in a strategic way. I know you've heard this before, but experience is a great teacher but only if you employ self- reflection. Investing the time to think about things through deeper lenses helps you to understand yourself better. When you better understand yourself, you become a better person and professional. So, cheers to using this journal to help you establish the habit of self-reflecting.

Self-Checks Ins

Throughout this journal you will find self-check ins. The self-check ins list the 8 primary emotions: anger, fear, joy, sadness, anticipation, surprise, trust, and disgust. The purpose of the self-check-ins are to help you to identify your emotions. Before each prompt you will have the opportunity to choose the emotion(s) you identify best with. This exercise encourages the habit of identifying your emotions which promotes emotional intelligence.

Emotional Intelligence is essential to maximizing your work experience. Emotional Intelligence is having the ability to identify and manage your emotions and being able to connect with others. Understanding where you are emotionally gives you the power to be more efficient in your work and establish effective relationships with colleagues/ clients.

Safe Space

Sometimes you just need a safe place to write freely about what's on your mind and that's exactly why this space was created. It's a no judgement zone. Many people take to their social media accounts to share what's on their mind but that is not always the best outlet. Honestly, social media is NOT a safe space for you to share your deepest, private thoughts. In this space you are free to write about anything you want regardless if it is related to work or your personal life.

How to use the safe space:

1. Silence your phone and put it out of sight.

2. Set a specific amount of time to allow yourself to write freely.

3. Try your best to write what comes to mind continuously during that time.

4. Don't worry about misspelled words or grammatical errors. Contrary to what you learned in English class, this space allows for it.

5. Remember you are not limited to write about a specific topic. In this space you can totally write one sentence about a topic and the next sentence can be totally about another topic. That's the beauty of having safe space to write.

6. Have FUN!

The Random Acts of Kindness Challenge

Practicing gratitude is like having a gift that keeps on giving. I've learned that practicing gratitude compels me to give to others more. Throughout this journal you will find the Random Acts of Kindness Challenge. The challenges were strategically designed to challenge you to show kindness in the workplace. This places you in the position to be a difference maker! Many workplaces lack having a culture of kindness but you can start it at your work place. You will be amazed at how showing kindness to others improves your mood and overall work day. And of course, when you take on the challenge, you will have an opportunity to self-reflect by journaling what you experienced through the challenge.

About This Journal

This journal is unique in that it is strategically infused with self-care techniques such as gratitude, self-reflection, random acts of kindness, inspirational quotes, and safe writing spaces to help you establish the habit of identifying the perks in the work that you do. I've used this tool professionally and it has helped me to maintain a positive perspective about the work that I do. It has also increased my morale, work productivity, and overall creativity. Your creativity will be awakened which will allow you to think beyond and create opportunities for you to shine in your work.

This journal contains 21 self-reflective, gratitude inducing prompts plus more. Why 21 prompts? I strategically created 21 prompts for this journal because it has been found that practicing gratitude for 21 days can lead to up 180 days of optimism.

How to use this journal:

1. Silence your phone and put it out of sight.

2. Set a time of day to write in your journal. Just like you schedule doctor's appointments, meetings with clients, etc. It is important for you to schedule an appointment with your journal. Remember, the time you commit to journaling is an investment.

3. *If you are journaling while at work, schedule your journaling

during one of your breaks or designate a time at the beginning or end or your work day.

4. Set a time allotment. How long do you plan to journal? If you are a beginner don't let this intimidate you. Simply, start by allowing yourself at least 10 to 15 minutes to journal. If you're having a challenging day allow yourself more time. Use a timer via your smartphone if needed.

5. Get your favorite pen or pencil. Try to designate this writing utensil for journaling only. You will be amazed at how having a pen or pencil that you love will encourage you to write freely.

6. Identify a special place to journal. For some, it's useful to journal while at work. Is there a place at work that inspires you? It could be your office, break room, employee lounge, outside, etc. If you do not have a place that inspires you, don't let this stop you, be creative and designate a space.

7. Now that you're all set. It's time to write and reflect. Take a moment to read the prompt. Reflect on the prompt and allow your thoughts to flow.

Self Check-In

Identify Your Current Emotion(s)

☐	Joy😄	☐	Disgust😖
☐	Anger😣	☐	Surprised😲
☐	Sad😢	☐	Fear😦
☐	Trust😁	☐	Anticipation😫

Safe Space

What's on your mind?

_____

_____

_____

_____

_____

_____

_____

_____

_____

_____

_____

_____

_____

_____

_____

How we begin our day at work sets the tone and pace for the day.

Begin your workday with intentionality.

How do you **begin** your work day? Name something you can **intentionally do** that will positively **inspire** your work day. How would this inspire **you** and **others**?

_____

_____

_____

_____

_____

_____

_____

_____

_____

_____

_____

_____

_____

_____

_____

_____

_____

_____

Self Check-In

Identify Your Current Emotion(s)

☐ Joy😄   ☐ Disgust☹️

☐ Anger😫   ☐ Surprised😲

☐ Sad😢   ☐ Fear😨

☐ Trust😁   ☐ Anticipation😬

Safe Space

What's on your mind?

_____

_____

_____

_____

_____

_____

_____

_____

_____

_____

_____

_____

_____

_____

_____

_____

Gratitude gives you the power to make an ordinary day extraordinary.

What did you do today that you enjoyed? Finish this sentence: **Today**, I am **grateful** for being able to **enjoy**...

_____

_____

_____

_____

_____

_____

_____

_____

_____

_____

_____

_____

_____

_____

_____

_____

_____

_____

_____

_____

Self Check-In

Identify Your Current Emotion(s)

☐ Joy😄   ☐ Disgust😖

☐ Anger😣   ☐ Surprised😲

☐ Sad😢   ☐ Fear😧

☐ Trust🤗   ☐ Anticipation😫

Safe Space

What's on your mind?

_____

_____

_____

_____

_____

_____

_____

_____

_____

_____

_____

_____

_____

_____

_____

_____

Celebrating the WINS will keep you motivated during challenging times.

A **WIN** is an accomplishment you have achieved either professionally and/or personally.

Talk about a **WIN** in your professional/ personal life that have brought you the most **happiness**. How did you celebrate this **WIN**?

_____

_____

_____

_____

_____

_____

_____

_____

_____

_____

_____

_____

_____

_____

_____

_____

_____

_____

Self Check-In

Identify Your Current Emotion(s)

- [ ] Joy😄
- [ ] Anger😡
- [ ] Sad😢
- [ ] Trust😁
- [ ] Disgust😕
- [ ] Surprised😲
- [ ] Fear😨
- [ ] Anticipation😬

Safe Space

What's on your mind?

_____

_____

_____

_____

_____

_____

_____

_____

_____

_____

_____

_____

_____

_____

_____

A dream is a foreshadow of what is attainable. A dream becomes a WIN when you commit to making it a reality.

Talk about the **next WIN** you are anticipating. What are you doing now to make this **WIN** a **reality**? What **progress** have you made thus far that makes you most **proud**?

_____

_____

_____

_____

_____

_____

_____

_____

_____

_____

_____

_____

_____

_____

_____

_____

_____

Random Act of Kindness Challenge:

TODAY, compliment three colleagues on their WINS (accomplishments).

Random Act of Kindness Reflections

Who did you compliment today?

_____

_____

_____

_____

_____

What were their reactions to your compliment?

_____

_____

_____

_____

How did complimenting them make you feel?

_____

_____

_____

_____

_____

Self Check-In

Identify Your Current Emotion(s)

☐ Joy😄   ☐ Disgust😖

☐ Anger😣   ☐ Surprised😲

☐ Sad😢   ☐ Fear😦

☐ Trust😬   ☐ Anticipation😫

Safe Space

What's on your mind?

_____

_____

_____

_____

_____

_____

_____

_____

_____

_____

_____

_____

_____

_____

_____

Unless someone like you cares a whole awful lot, nothing is going to get better. It's not.''

–Dr. Seuss, The Lorax

Advocacy can be challenging and hard but it can also be rewarding.

Describe a time in which you had to **advocate** for a customer/ client. Was your stance for advocacy supported by the majority or the minority? What did you **learn** about **yourself** personally and professionally from this experience?

_____

_____

_____

_____

_____

_____

_____

_____

_____

_____

_____

_____

_____

_____

Self Check-In

Identify Your Current Emotion(s)

☐ Joy😄   ☐ Disgust🙁

☐ Anger😬   ☐ Surprised😲

☐ Sad🥺   ☐ Fear😦

☐ Trust😁   ☐ Anticipation😖

Safe Space

What's on your mind?

_____

_____

_____

_____

_____

_____

_____

_____

_____

_____

_____

_____

_____

_____

_____

_____

_____

Learning to enjoy the moments that our current work affords us is important. Early in my career, while working a challenging position, I often thought about what life would be like when I changed positions. To be honest, I forgot to savor the current moments, the colleagues and clients I was afforded to meet, lessons learned, partnerships made, etc. When I finally changed positions, I actually missed many of the things that I enjoyed most about that challenging position. I wholeheartedly believe that if I had stopped to "smell the roses" and enjoy the perks of that challenging position, it would have made the days sweeter.

What do you **enjoy** most about the current **work** that you do and why?

_____

_____

_____

_____

_____

_____

_____

_____

_____

_____

_____

_____

_____

_____

_____

_____

_____

_____

_____

Self Check-In

Identify Your Current Emotion(s)

☐ Joy😄   ☐ Disgust😖

☐ Anger😫   ☐ Surprised😮

☐ Sad😢   ☐ Fear😨

☐ Trust🤗   ☐ Anticipation😬

Safe Space

What's on your mind?

_____

_____

_____

_____

_____

_____

_____

_____

_____

_____

_____

_____

_____

_____

_____

_____

_____

We've all had our fair share of challenging clients/ customers/ situations. In hindsight, it's the client's that challenged me the most for which I am grateful. Challenging clients require personal and professional self-reflection. The clients/ customers that challenge us the most challenge helps us to evolve. For each challenging client I have had to serve, I can truly say that I have grown. Whether it was growth in tolerance, a lesson learned about setting appropriate boundaries, etc. I GREW and it has helped to shape the professional and person that I am today.

Discuss the most **challenging** client, customer, or situation you've faced as a professional. What did you **learn** about **yourself** both professionally and personally? How has this experience **strengthened** you as a professional?

_____

_____

_____

_____

_____

_____

_____

_____

_____

_____

_____

_____

_____

_____

_____

_____

_____

_____

Random Act of Kindness Challenge

Send 3 people an encouraging message today. The message can be sent via phone, voicemail, text message, email, or etc.

Random Act of Kindness Reflections

To whom did you decide to send an encouraging message?

_____

_____

_____

Why them? What made you choose those individuals?

_____

_____

_____

What were their reactions?

_____

_____

_____

How did encouraging them make you feel?

_____

_____

_____

Self Check-In

Identify Your Current Emotion(s)

☐ Joy😄   ☐ Disgust😖

☐ Anger😣   ☐ Surprised😮

☐ Sad🥺   ☐ Fear😨

☐ Trust🤗   ☐ Anticipation😬

Safe Space

What's on your mind?

_____

_____

_____

_____

_____

_____

_____

_____

_____

_____

_____

_____

_____

_____

_____

_____

_____

_____

Vision is vital. Without vision, it is difficult to find purpose and joy in the work that you are currently doing. As a professional, I have learned that it is important to have a vision of where I am aiming to go and who I aim to become.

Write a letter to your professional self **10 years** in the **future**. What do you **foresee** to be **different** about the work that you do 10 years from today? What do you **perceive** to have **accomplished**? What lessons would you like to say that you've learned?

_____

_____

_____

_____

_____

_____

_____

_____

_____

_____

_____

_____

_____

_____

_____

_____

_____

Self Check-In

Identify Your Current Emotion(s)

☐ Joy😄

☐ Anger😣

☐ Sad😢

☐ Trust😁

☐ Disgust😖

☐ Surprised😲

☐ Fear😟

☐ Anticipation😬

Safe Space

What's on your mind?

_____

_____

_____

_____

_____

_____

_____

_____

_____

_____

_____

_____

_____

_____

_____

_____

_____

Taking risks has rewards.
Regardless of the outcome, you
will be proud and wiser.

Write about a **risk** that was very hard for you to take as a professional, but you **did** it **anyway**? What **lessons** did you learn from this experience? How has this experience made you **grateful**?

_____
_____
_____
_____
_____
_____
_____
_____
_____
_____
_____
_____
_____
_____
_____
_____
_____
_____
_____

Self Check-In

Identify Your Current Emotion(s)

☐ Joy😆   ☐ Disgust😖

☐ Anger😣   ☐ Surprised😲

☐ Sad😢   ☐ Fear😨

☐ Trust😁   ☐ Anticipation😖

Safe Space

What's on your mind?

_____

_____

_____

_____

_____

_____

_____

_____

_____

_____

_____

_____

_____

_____

_____

_____

_____

Compliments amplify our strengths. They confirm what you already know about yourself.

What is the best **compliment** you have ever received professionally, personally, or both? What makes this compliment so **meaningful** to you? What did this compliment **teach** you about yourself?

_____

_____

_____

_____

_____

_____

_____

_____

_____

_____

_____

_____

_____

_____

_____

_____

_____

_____

_____

Random Act of Kindness Challenge

Write a kind message to yourself and leave it in a high traffic place (such as your work desk/ station, the steering wheel in your car, in your wallet, and/or on your mirror).

Random Act of Kindness Reflections

Was it difficult to write a kind message to yourself? Why or Why not?

_____
_____
_____
_____

When writing the message, where you speaking more to your professional self, personal self, or both? Why?

_____
_____
_____
_____

Write the kind message that you wrote to yourself below:

_____
_____
_____
_____

Self Check-In

Identify Your Current Emotion(s)

☐ Joy😁   ☐ Disgust😖

☐ Anger😣   ☐ Surprised😲

☐ Sad😢   ☐ Fear😧

☐ Trust😬   ☐ Anticipation😖

Safe Space

What's on your mind?

_____

_____

_____

_____

_____

_____

_____

_____

_____

_____

_____

_____

_____

_____

_____

_____

Understanding what motivates you gives you the power to refuel. What motivates us most far exceeds material possessions. Motivation is all around you.

What **motivates** you the **most** about the **work** that you do? How does it **refuel** you as a **professional**?

_____

_____

_____

_____

_____

_____

_____

_____

_____

_____

_____

_____

_____

_____

_____

_____

_____

_____

_____

Self Check-In

Identify Your Current Emotion(s)

☐ Joy😄   ☐ Disgust😧

☐ Anger😠   ☐ Surprised😮

☐ Sad😢   ☐ Fear😖

☐ Trust😁   ☐ Anticipation😬

Safe Space

What's on your mind?

_____

_____

_____

_____

_____

_____

_____

_____

_____

_____

_____

_____

_____

_____

_____

_____

_____

_____

What's a Superpower?

Everyone has a Superpower. A superpower is a special gift/talent you possess that benefits others and you. When you are afforded the opportunity to use your superpower, it fuels your sense of purpose.

What's your **superpower**? How do you **utilize** your **superpower** in the work that you do every day? How has your **superpower helped others**? How has it given you a sense of **purpose**?

_____

_____

_____

_____

_____

_____

_____

_____

_____

_____

_____

_____

_____

_____

_____

_____

_____

_____

Self Check-In

Identify Your Current Emotion(s)

☐ Joy😄

☐ Anger😣

☐ Sad😢

☐ Trust😭

☐ Disgust😖

☐ Surprised😲

☐ Fear😟

☐ Anticipation😬

Safe Space

What's on your mind?

_____

_____

_____

_____

_____

_____

_____

_____

_____

_____

_____

_____

_____

_____

_____

_____

Laughter makes the day come ALIVE. Finding the humor in things we cannot control is powerful.

Describe one of your **funniest** moments/ experiences at work? Who was involved and **what happened**? Be sure to take your time with this one and enjoy the **humor**.

_____

_____

_____

_____

_____

_____

_____

_____

_____

_____

_____

_____

_____

_____

_____

_____

_____

_____

_____

_____

_____

Random Act of Kindness Challenge

Write a note of gratitude to a person you feel is often overlooked at your workplace.

Random Acts of Kindness Reflections

To whom did you write the note?

_____

_____

How is this person an asset to your workplace?

_____

_____

Did you give the note to the person? What was the person's reaction to the note?

_____

_____

How did this act of kindness make you feel?

_____

_____

Self Check-In

Identify Your Current Emotion(s)

☐ Joy😄 ☐ Disgust😕

☐ Anger😣 ☐ Surprised😮

☐ Sad😢 ☐ Fear😧

☐ Trust😁 ☐ Anticipation😬

Safe Space

What's on your mind?

_____

_____

_____

_____

_____

_____

_____

_____

_____

_____

_____

_____

_____

_____

_____

_____

Surround yourself with people

that *inspire* you.

Inspiration is the power that compels us to become

who we dream to be.

The person that inspires you the most

served as a reflection of your values and beliefs.

Who is the most **inspiring** person you know? What **qualities** do you **admire** most about them?

_____

_____

_____

_____

_____

_____

_____

_____

_____

_____

_____

_____

_____

_____

_____

_____

_____

_____

_____

Self Check-In

Identify Your Current Emotion(s)

☐ Joy😄   ☐ Disgust😖

☐ Anger😣   ☐ Surprised😲

☐ Sad😢   ☐ Fear😨

☐ Trust😁   ☐ Anticipation😖

Safe Space

What's on your mind?

_____
_____
_____
_____
_____
_____
_____
_____
_____
_____
_____
_____
_____
_____
_____
_____
_____

"And in the end, it's not the years

in your life that count,

It's the LIFE in your years."

-Abraham Lincoln

What's something that you are **grateful** to **have** today that you did not have one year ago?

_____

_____

_____

_____

_____

_____

_____

_____

_____

_____

_____

_____

_____

_____

_____

_____

_____

_____

_____

Self Check-In

Identify Your Current Emotion(s)

☐ Joy😄   ☐ Disgust😖

☐ Anger😤   ☐ Surprised😲

☐ Sad😢   ☐ Fear😨

☐ Trust😁   ☐ Anticipation😬

Safe Space

What's on your mind?

_____

_____

_____

_____

_____

_____

_____

_____

_____

_____

_____

_____

_____

_____

_____

_____

_____

_____

_____

In a world that glorifies extroversion, it is important to know how you work best. For some extroverts, you may find that you work best in groups, while introverts may work best solo. Neither is bad or taboo. The world needs introverts, extroverts, and ambiverts (those with qualities of both the introvert and extrovert). There is power in knowing what works best for you. Knowing what works best for you helps to capitalize on your strengths and prepare in the areas in need of growth. Know your power and use it.

If you had the choice to **work** with **others** (in a group) or to work **alone**, which would you choose? Why? Do you **work best** in groups or do you work best alone? How has this **helped** in the work that you do? What do you **like** or **dislike** the most about working in groups? What do you **like** or **dislike** about working alone?

_____

_____

_____

_____

_____

_____

_____

_____

_____

_____

_____

_____

_____

_____

_____

_____

_____

_____

Random Act of Kindness Challenge

Catch a colleague doing something great today and brag about them to their supervisor/ leader.

Remember to brag to your colleague's supervisor/leader.

Random Act of Kindness Reflections

What noble act did your colleague perform and why was it important?

_____

_____

What was the supervisor's/ leader's response?

_____

_____

Did you tell your colleague you bragged on them? Why or why not?

_____

_____

What was your colleague's reaction to learning that someone bragged on them?

_____

_____

Self Check-In

Identify Your Current Emotion(s)

☐ Joy😄   ☐ Disgust😖

☐ Anger😣   ☐ Surprised😲

☐ Sad😢   ☐ Fear😨

☐ Trust😁   ☐ Anticipation😬

Safe Space

What's on your mind?

_____
_____
_____
_____
_____
_____
_____
_____
_____
_____
_____
_____
_____
_____
_____

Your work environment is vital to success. It is important that your work environment motivates you to grow and achieve success.

Describe your work **environment** physically. Does it **inspire** you? Is it uplifting? What is something you can do to add **positivity/ inspiration** to your current **workspace**?

_____

_____

_____

_____

_____

_____

_____

_____

_____

_____

_____

_____

_____

_____

_____

_____

_____

_____

_____

Self Check-In

Identify Your Current Emotion(s)

☐ Joy😄　　☐ Disgust😖

☐ Anger😫　　☐ Surprised😲

☐ Sad😢　　☐ Fear😟

☐ Trust😁　　☐ Anticipation😖

Safe Space

What's on your mind?

_____

_____

_____

_____

_____

_____

_____

_____

_____

_____

_____

_____

_____

_____

_____

Life is busy. If we are not careful, we will find ourselves engulfed in the busyness of life ignoring our personal needs. Whatever you ignore, will get louder and inevitably become a nuisance. The best way to pay yourself is not with money or tangible things; the best way you can pay yourself is with ATTENTION. Pay attention to your needs.

Finish this statement:

"I could **really use** some_____(insert something intangible) right now." How would receiving this **positively affect** your day and mood?

_____
_____
_____
_____
_____
_____
_____
_____
_____
_____
_____
_____
_____
_____
_____
_____
_____
_____
_____

Random Act of Kindness Challenge

Thinking about the intangible gift that you wrote about in the previous pages; name a person you know that could use the same intangible gift. When you are able, consider giving the exact intangible gift that you need to that person.

Random Acts of Kindness Reflections

What intangible gift did you give?

_____
_____
_____

To whom did you give it to and why?

_____
_____
_____

What was the person's reaction?

_____
_____
_____

How did their reaction make you feel?

_____
_____
_____

Self Check-In

Identify Your Current Emotion(s)

☐ Joy😄   ☐ Disgust☹️

☐ Anger😣   ☐ Surprised😲

☐ Sad😥   ☐ Fear😨

☐ Trust😁   ☐ Anticipation😖

Safe Space

What's on your mind?

_____

_____

_____

_____

_____

_____

_____

_____

_____

_____

_____

_____

_____

_____

_____

_____

_____

Reflection is one of the best gifts you can gift to yourself. It compels you to think about your experiences and identify the lessons learned. The lessons learned help to prepare you for your next anticipated level.

Knowing what you know now, if you could give **advice** to your younger self **10 years ago** what would the advice be? Why?

_____

_____

_____

_____

_____

_____

_____

_____

_____

_____

_____

_____

_____

_____

_____

_____

_____

_____

_____

Self Check-In

Identify Your Current Emotion(s)

☐ Joy😄   ☐ Disgust😟

☐ Anger😣   ☐ Surprised😲

☐ Sad😢   ☐ Fear😨

☐ Trust😇   ☐ Anticipation😖

Safe Space

What's on your mind?

_____

_____

_____

_____

_____

_____

_____

_____

_____

_____

_____

_____

_____

_____

_____

_____

_____

Let the victories

of others

inspire you to succeed.

Write about a time your client or colleague experienced a **victory**. How did their **victory** make you feel? How did the **victory inspire** you?

_____

_____

_____

_____

_____

_____

_____

_____

_____

_____

_____

_____

_____

_____

_____

_____

_____

_____

_____

_____

Self Check-In

Identify Your Current Emotion(s)

☐ Joy😄	☐ Disgust🙁
☐ Anger😣	☐ Surprised😲
☐ Sad😟	☐ Fear😨
☐ Trust😁	☐ Anticipation😬

Safe Space

What's on your mind?

_____
_____
_____
_____
_____
_____
_____
_____
_____
_____
_____
_____
_____
_____
_____
_____
_____

Working with challenging people can be rewarding. Some of the most self-aware moments I've experienced while at work can be contributed to having to work with people who are "not so easy" to work with. The more I worked with them on projects, deadlines, etc; the more I was forced to learn about my values. In retrospect, I am thankful for the opportunities given to work with those individuals because in the process I learned so much about myself.

We've all had our share of our Challenging colleagues and/or bosses. Talk about an instance in which you had to work with a **challenging** colleague or boss. What did you **learn** most about **yourself**? How has working with this person contributed to your personal/ professional **growth**?

_____
_____
_____
_____
_____
_____
_____
_____
_____
_____
_____
_____
_____
_____
_____
_____
_____
_____

Random Act of Kindness Challenge

Think about one of the hardest working individuals at your workplace. You know the one that works long hours and often stays late to make sure the job gets done. Invite them to take a break.

Random Acts of Kindness Reflections

Who did you choose for this random act of kindness and why?

_____
_____
_____
_____

Did they join you for a break when offered?

_____
_____
_____
_____

How did this act of kindness make you feel?

_____
_____
_____
_____

Author Bio

Terricka Hardy, is a Licensed Clinical Social Worker, therapist, dynamic speaker, national trainer, and motivator. An inspiring person by nature, Terricka has dedicated her life works to helping individuals overcome. She has affected lasting positive changes in the lives of many

Terricks is an appointed member of the National Association of Social Workers (NASW) National Ethics Committee, Memphis VA Social Work Professional Standards Board member, and Board Certified Diplomate in Clinical Social Work. She is a published author of two books *I Prosper Daily,* a daily devotional, and *The Self-Care A-Z Adult Coloring; both available on amazon.com.* Terricka has assisted in revising the NASW Policy Statement on Professional Impairment and is a featured co-author of *The Routledge Handbook of Social Work Ethics and Values* textbook published in 2019.

Terricka has trained numerous of professional and community groups about mental health recovery, burnout, and self-care. She is devoted to enhancing the human well-being not only for clients but also for Social Workers and other allied professionals. Terricka firmly believes that in order to best service clients and uphold ethical standards, you must invest in self-care. Terricka provides employee resilience and self-care tools for professionals.

Through engagement, education, and empowerment Terricka seeks to influence positive change in communities, individuals, employees, and programs. Contact Terricka today to be a speaker at your next event and/or to assist you with your programming and staff needs at thardylcsw@yahoo.com.

Made in the USA
Las Vegas, NV
31 October 2023